HAPPY CAKES

By

James Williams

Special Note To My Readers

Dear Reader,

This book is uniquely designed to be good for you and it has many lessons for people of all ages. I hope you enjoy this book as much as I have enjoyed writing it.

This book will be like the following:

1. Eating your favorite meal at your surprise birthday party surrounded by all the people you love and that love you followed by a weekend sleepover at a resort on the beach on a holiday weekend.
2. Hearing the words "I love you" for the first time all over again.
3. Someone sharing a gift with you in a time of your great need and asking for nothing in return.
4. You showing courage and being a great friend to someone who needs help and asking for nothing in return.
5. Waking up early only to realize that it is a holiday and that you don't have school or work and you fall easily back to sleep for another 5 hours.

I hope you enjoy this story and share it with your friends. I look forward to meeting you and discussing this book with you at a local reading. Thank you!

Sincerely,

James Williams

On Sunday morning, a week before Christmas, Leyla woke up slowly and 5 miles away at Aaron's house, he woke up slowly. Both woke up around the same time but both were totally unaware of this fact. Their actions mirrored each other as if they were puppets connected with the same strings from the same invisible puppet master even though they were 5 miles away from each other...their rooms were very still and quiet, and slightly dark with a small sliver of the morning sun light peaking over the top of the curtains in their rooms, their hands were by their sides outside the tucked covers....slowly, very slowly they opened their eyes as a small tear ran down both sides of their faces....they slowly looked up through watery eyes to see "the" picture......not just any picture.... this picture reminded them of one of the happiest days of their lives....this picture had a name...and its name was Happy Cakes....... With it being a week before Christmas, one of the happiest seasons of the year, they wondered how they found themselves so unhappy and crying in their beds....Leyla and Aaron slowly started to think about the last 5 months when their lives were so much different....

Five months prior, during the month of August, when school had started back, Leyla had just gotten her books out of her locker and she was heading to her next class, Art. Leyla was a pretty girl with soft brown eyes, long flowing dark hair with the girl-next-door type of face. Her voice was soft and had a melodic rhythm and tone when she spoke. Although she was a nice young lady with a soft voice, she had an assertive manner and the ability to speak up when situation required it. Like when some kid in her class kept kicking her desk, she spoke up immediately and loud putting the kid on the spot and he stopped. She wasn't an attention seeker nor did she try standout amongst the other girls of similar age. She wasn't flashy with her mannerisms or gestures, loud or drew attention to herself. She wasn't critical of those that did that but it just wasn't her style. Her parents considered her very mature for her age and they loved the fact that she could maintain her grades, and extracurricular activities with no problems. She had friends, who were not exactly like her, but they were good kids and they were themselves around Leyla. Her personality put them at ease and allowed them to not pretend to be someone they were not. Leyla was gentle in every way possible but inside she was a ball of energy with laser like focus. She could focus so intently on projects, objects, and situations that sometimes she didn't notice anything going on around her. This laser-like focus allowed her to be a great chess player. She loved chess, every part of it, the strategy, planning and the ability to maintain focus for hours. Her father was a chess player and he had introduced it to her when she was young. She loved the time spent with him as well as the time she spent playing chess. She really loved the fact that when she played she didn't have to rely upon anyone just herself. She was in the 9th grade and her local high school was called Ridge High School. As Leyla was entering her Art class, her thoughts were on what was this exciting project that Mrs. Berry had been mentioning the last few weeks.

Aaron, who was in the same Art class as Leyla, was already in class and had already taken his seat. Aaron had dark hair with brown eyes. He was not bad looking, rather, he looked like a nice guy who could make logical decisions. He was a student-athlete but he wasn't a loud jock-type. He carried himself in a mature manner well beyond his years. As a tennis player, he had a quiet confidence about himself and that confidence served him well during his tennis matches against higher ranked or older players. His parents were proud of his accomplishments as a student-athlete but they were prouder that he was able to balance school work and his extracurricular activity. He was organized and this helped him to carefully allot his time to practice and to his studies. As he was waiting in his Art class, he was thinking about a girl in his class that he had known since kindergarten, Leyla. When he saw Leyla entering the class, he thought she was pretty, confident and cool as well. He wasn't attracted to loud girls or those that wanted to be the center of attention. Although they had been in school together for years, when he saw her now, he saw her differently. It was like she transformed into a young lady during the summer. He wasn't sure why now he decided to talk to her about going out but here he was deciding how he would ask her out. He already knew her from kindergarten and in middle school they had been "friends". Meaning, they knew each other and chatted at different times but he never asked her out. Today, he thought she seemed extremely pretty. Her hair was down that day, she wore a white blouse and a pair of blue jeans with brown sandals. Her thin gold necklace was shiny and drew attention to her face. This day, Leyla had chosen to wear her hair down so it fell softly in her face, across her right eye to be exact. As Aaron watched her walk in the class, he wondered how he would approach the subject of going on a date with Leyla. He wasn't worried about rejection, he was more worried about looking like a fool when he asked. He didn't want to be like those guys in the movies stumbling over words, and acting like they were shy, which he wasn't. He decided upon the "I need help" technique. This was a gentle approach to asking someone out by humbling yourself and asking for help. He thought to himself what he would need help with that allow him to ask her out since they only had one class together. Mrs. Berry's art project would present an opportunity for but Aaron was totally unaware of this potential opportunity. He decided would think about it and wait until after Art class to approach her.

Use the all tools at your disposal, all of the resources available to you, enlist the help of others and use the most vibrant colors, to create the life you want. Remember, you are the artist- James Williams

Today in Art class, Mrs. Berry was very excited about today's art project. She had given the student hints the last few weeks and they seemed eager to hear about the new project. She could barely get the words out to explain the project, which seemed complicated on the surface, but it was fun and cool. It was a four-week project or at least they had four weeks to complete and turn it in. At the three-week mark, they had to check in and provide the status of the project and say how well it was going. If you were done with the project, you could turn it in. At the four-week mark, the project had to be turned in and displayed in the art class for a week. The art class project had two parts to it. First, the students had to make something. It didn't matter if it was an object, food, toy or clothing. Second, they had to draw and paint the picture of the object on a canvass or paper. For example, if you made a clay cup, design it however you like and then draw it and paint it. This was a unique project but what made it even more interesting was that she allowed them to have a partner. One of the rules was that each person had to do their "fair" share to the greatest extent possible. So, if one made it, then the other painted it or vice versa or you did everything together but one person shouldn't do everything no matter how artistic they were. Sounded simple to everyone. Now, the only hard part was to find a partner. Mrs. Berry felt the team concept to the project was a bit unique and it was encouraged as art was meant to be shared and what better way to share it than by working with someone on an art project. This was the perfect opportunity for Aaron, who wasn't exactly artsy, to work with someone and that someone could be Leyla. In this class, Leyla didn't have any true friends and the class was nearly half boys and half girls. There was no one that she really talked to this class and with the previous art projects, all work was done alone. So, she thought it was odd when the teacher decided for them to have partners but figured it would be cool to work with a partner. The students had five minutes to find a partner in class- starting NOW! Aaron knew immediately that this was his perfect opportunity to talk to and work with Leyla. He went directly to Leyla. "Need a partner" he asked. She nodded with little enthusiasm. She wasn't sure what kind of partner he would make but figured he was a nice guy, and he would at least pull his weight and do his part. What could it hurt plus there wasn't anyone that she really wanted to work with. Selecting a partner was the easy part, no matter how awkward it was for the 9th graders to ask someone to be your partner, finding time to work together and agree on something would prove to be a challenge for all of them.

Interpreting art is easy, and fun; working together on an art project takes art- James Williams

As the school year rolled into September, Aaron and Leyla were partners now working on their unique art project of creating or making something, drawing it and painting a picture of it. It was both artsy and crafty or crafty and artsy. Leyla and Aaron both shared the same view of this unique project although both entered into this partnership with different perspectives of the partnership. Aaron saw it as an opportunity to get to know and ask out Leyla while Leyla saw it as another school project that required cooperation and a sense of team work with one of her fellow students. Both were sure in their minds they could it done and get a good grade.

There would be challenges for them to work together as with any two people working together on a project. Although they talked a little about it during Art class, time was their major challenge, as they were not allowed that much of class time to work on the project. The second challenge would be deciding upon what object they would create. For now, time was the major issue. Leyla had chess club which met pretty frequently during the week to play and discuss strategy and tactics. For Aaron, he had tennis practice nearly every day except Fridays. To get around the time issue, they decided to exchange cell phone numbers and communicate via texts and on the phone at night time when they had time. In just a short few days, the texts were confusing with suggestions and ideas. For example, Leyla suggested they create a piece of pottery and the discussion turned to pigs wearing shorts. Funny, right? Despite the confusing text messages, they had a lot of good ideas and the phone conversations helped to clarify the weird and funny texts and helped both to relax after a long day of school and practices. They found their conversations very easy, logical and often drifted into other areas of their life such as where are you from, do you have pets, and the most basic question that really had a positive impression upon Leyla was "How was your day?" To Leyla, that simple question meant more than just tell me about your day, it meant "I'm going to listen while you talk and I'm sincerely interested in knowing about your day". They talked for hours about her day which in her mind wasn't that exciting or interesting. Most people think their days aren't that interesting or exciting until you start talking about the details of your day. For example, you may talk about getting ready for school and as you discuss what you do to get ready, you may mention whether or not you are a morning person, what you normally eat, and how you get to school. These simple and honest conversations lead the two teens into discussions about their personalities, likes and dislikes and family structure. During these conversations, they found they had so much in common. They both were morning-types, they both rode the bus but got rides when they were running late and both were light breakfast eaters. With so many things in common, they found themselves wanting and waiting to talk to each other….they missed each other when they were not able to talk although they never said that to each other. The texts seemed so cold and distant compared to the warm, funny and interesting phone conversations. Sometimes the topic about their lives would dominate the conversation and they would only have a few mins to discuss their project. It was Leyla who suggested they meet on Saturday at the library to really dig deep into their project. She maintained her list of school assignments and her laser-like focus and organizational skills reminded her that she had something due that needed to get done. Aaron eagerly agreed to meet her at the local library that Saturday morning.

The Saturday morning that greeted them was bright, clear and sunny and both were looking forward to seeing each other. Since both were organized and responsible, they were there a little before 9am as planned and they were among the first ones inside as the library opened. Both found the polite, warm conversations from the phone at night transferred very nicely to the face to face. Seeing her laugh at his jokes or witty comments warmed his heart and really drew him closer to her. For Leyla, she observed how mature he was, much more mature than the boys in their grade or 10th grade. He really listened when she talked and he respected what she said. As they gazed at each other, they had to remind each other of why they were there.....to work on the project. After 30 to 40 minutes of small talk, they turned their focus on their project. With laser-like focus, Leyla presented her ideas for the project and welcomed the thoughts, ideas and feedback from Aaron. He presented his ideas and Leyla listen to see if there were any that would make her change her mind. Nope, not one. This would be their first and only discussion where they didn't agree on something. For the next hour, ideas were kicked around and what kept coming up was what do they create? What could they create together and then draw and paint a picture of it? What they decided upon made both laugh uncontrollably. They laughed so hard that other people in the library started staring at them. Like two kids eating cookies out of the cookie jar when the parent's head was turned, they giggled in the cutest manner as they settled upon cupcakes with smiley faces called Happy Cakes. It was so funny that Leyla had tears in her eyes and Aaron's stomach muscles started to hurt. They laughed for so hard and for so long, they began to look very closely at each other's face and for the first time, they truly saw each other. This moment would be the turning point in the friendship...from friendship to relationship. They would look back on this moment and remember.

Now that they decided what they would do, they started working out the details. First, they needed the supplies and a place to make them. They were not going to waste too much time on whether they were chocolate or vanilla rather they wanted to make them, decorate them, draw and paint them and eat them. They presented the project to their parents and they agreed it was a good, fun project. Besides the fact that their parents concurred with the selected project, the other good news was that Leyla had most of the supplies to make cupcakes but she didn't have the frosting and other decorations but she would get those and Aaron would get the art supplies. So, they decided to use her cupcake mix and Aaron would purchase the art supplies. Next, was where to make the cupcakes, whose home? They decided to use Leyla's home. They checked their families' schedules and personal schedules and they were clear. This was awesome. They would be able to work together on the project, see each other and more importantly for Aaron, he would be able to spend time with Leyla and meet Leyla's family.

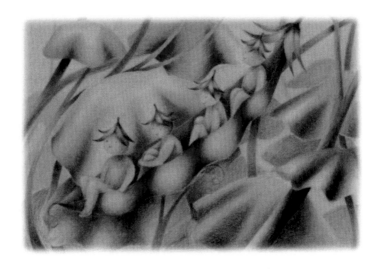

Family- Like peas in a pod, the more we spend time together, the more we love and enjoy each other- James Williams

Aaron's family consisted of his mother Vanna, father Robert and younger sister Mary by 3 years. As they sat around on Friday evening before the Saturday that Aaron was going to Leyla's house, the subject of the project came up casually and then became a little tense. Aaron's mom, Vanna, was the one that brought up the subject as she was the one who purchased the art supplies for Aaron as well the one dropping Aaron off at Leyla's house on Saturday. She asked Aaron, "Are you ready for tomorrow?" Aaron, who was aware the question wasn't very specific, asked for clarification of the question by responding "what?" which caused his father, Robert, to smile as his son stalled for more time.

Vanna pressed, "You know, are you ready to work on the project, do you need more supplies and how well do you think you will do cooking the cupcakes, oops, I mean Happy Cakes?" Here we go again thought Aaron, the interrogation to find out if there was more going on. He really wasn't ready to share his feelings about Leyla and the project was, well, a project. The only thing that made this project special to Aaron was the fact that Leyla was involved with it. Since his mother pressed, it seemed like everyone drew silent waiting on his response. In his typical Aaron fashion, he paused and thought he would focus on the things that weren't too close to his feelings, the art supplies. "Yes, I have everything I need and thank you again Mom for getting them for me", this seemed to Aaron like he was doing a good job of deflecting the question. He went further into details about the supplies, "Leyla has the frosting of different colors and flavors, and I have the art supplies". He decided to let them share in his excitement, just a little thinking it was safe with his younger sister around "and I think it is going to be so much fun" as he chuckled. Mary, his younger sister, couldn't resist the opening that Aaron presented her and she chimed in "Are you excited to work with Leyla, is she your girlfriend?" Aaron fumed inside at his sister as he squirmed slightly in his chair. He let his guard down for one second and Mary chimed in, prying for more information to embarrass him. He tried to deflect it before his parents picked up on it, "Girlfriend? Seriously? How do you go from school project to cupcakes to girlfriend?" His younger sister, who was smart, loved this type of fight in the front of the parents because she had absolutely nothing to lose and to see her older brother squirm caused her immense joy. She thought he deserved it just because he was a big brother and all big brothers deserved to be put on the spot in front of the parents at every opportunity. She wouldn't miss this opportunity and if she could, she would call the local news station and ask them to stick a microphone, lights and camera in his face and ask him even more prying questions. She thought to herself "squirm cupcake boy, squirm". She laughed inside at the thoughts as Aaron proceeded to shrug off her questions by saying "I have a great partner and we are going to work really hard tomorrow to finish as much as possible." He wanted to show his parents that he was responsible and serious about completing school projects. His dad, Robert, chimed in about Leyla, "who is your girl partner again and how do you know her and how did you two get to be partners?". Aaron went into the long story about the art project, Mrs. Berry requiring them to work together and how it was by "accident" or "just worked out" they got to be partners. He mentioned to them he had a great partner in Leyla and that he knew her from previous grades. He also shared she was smart and organized, which helped them a lot. Aaron was happy to be talking about this instead of responding to his sister's questions. As the conversation continued, Aaron left the room and started packing up his supplies and other things he would need for tomorrow and sat them by the door. Since it was going to relatively early arrival time, Aaron decided to go to bed early for him on Friday night. He didn't want to be tired the next day. He went about his normal routine and bid everyone a good night. While in the bed, he found it a little hard to sleep as he thought of Leyla and what her house looked like and how her parents would treat him and if she would be any different from when they were at school? These thoughts and questions raced through his mind and he figured it would be an absolute blast just to spend time with her no matter what happened as he drifted off to sleep.

At Leyla's house, on that same Friday night, similar events were happening. Unlike Aaron, she had a younger brother named Bobby. They looked very similar so it was easy for others to know they were related. Her father, Mike and her mother Pam were watching TV with Bobby as they heard Leyla in the kitchen setting out mixing bowls, batter box and other items needed for making the cupcakes. Leyla wanted everything to be ready and perfect when Aaron arrived. She was also planning to clean the kitchen again, even though it had been cleaned after dinner. She now knew how her mother felt when guests were coming over to their house. With so much energy and movement in the kitchen, her parents and brother couldn't help noticing her absence from the living room. Bobby was the first to speak up "Is Leyla's boyfriend coming over tomorrow?" Her parents laughed at the thought because no one ever said that especially Leyla. So, "Why did Bobby ask this question like that?" his parents thought. Her dad, Mike, was the first to chirp back to Bobby about his question, "It is a school project". Bobby, being a smarty pants said "Sure, and Leyla always cleans the kitchen after dinner and before we have guests on the same night?" His parents knew where he was going with it and decided to let Leyla defend herself and actions. "Leyla", her dad called from the living room. "Would you mind joining us in here" he continued. Fortunately, Leyla was almost done so she called back, "Just a minute please". She checked the area one last time and walked into the living room. "What's up" she asked as she entered the living room and sat down on the couch. She was aware of them having a conversation before her arrival but she didn't know what it was about and she figured they wanted her feedback or opinion on something. Her mom, Pam, decided to setup the conversation for Leyla so she would know what they were talking about. She trusted Leyla as Leyla has always been responsible and mature for her age and Leyla shared a lot with her mom as they had a good mother-daughter relationship. If this was a boyfriend, she figured Leyla would have shared that with her and the family before the invitation. "Leyla, we are talking about tomorrow when your classmate will be coming over to work on your school project and we were wondering who the young man is and what are the plans for tomorrow?" Leyla thought she had covered most, if not all, of the details but she knew her family very well. They were busy people who liked to confirm details especially when it involved guests and their home. Leyla didn't mind sharing details about the project or even the "guest", Aaron. To Leyla, he was a special guest but that wouldn't be shared with them, especially Bobby the brat. She mentioned Aaron's name and mentioned how funny it was that they chose cupcakes. Her brother sensing her parents were taking the conversation away from area he wanted it to go decided to chime in to guide it back to where he wanted. "So, is your boyfriend staying for dinner, I need to know if I need to set an extra place at the table?" Leyla shot "the look" at her younger brother and her eyes narrowed at him and she stared at him. It must have been a cold stare because her Dad chimed in to break the tension, "Now Bobby, be nice and don't assume". Leyla decided to ignore Bobby and the question and turned to her mom, "We should be done before dinner" and shot another look at Bobby. Bobby not content with her answer, decided to inquire about when they started dating and asked "So, will this be your first date?" Pam spoke up this time, "Bobby please, if they were dating, Leyla would have told us". After being dismissed by both parents, Bobby decided not to press his luck. He decided to focus on what he really wanted, cupcakes! "Will we be able to eat the cupcakes or is he taking them?" Leyla decided to respond to this question saying, "Don't know yet but don't worry, you will get at least one, dude." Seeming happy with that response, Bobby turned his attention back to the TV as Leyla explained the plans for Saturday to her parents. Her parents seemed genuinely interested and both would be there when Aaron arrived but Dad would probably leave at some point to take Bobby to his soccer game. The conversation lasted a few more minutes and Leyla decided she would get ready for bed. She hugged everyone and went to her room but not before she checked the kitchen one last time. While in her room, she wondered how Saturday would go and she desperately hoped Bobby wouldn't embarrass her. If her parents could keep Bobby busy and AWAY from the kitchen until his game, she figured Aaron and she could work together in peace. Her thoughts raced through the different scenarios as she drifted off to sleep.

Are you aware that we are staring at each other?-
James Williams

As the Saturday morning sun slowly rose, it was met by a young man who had been up for about 2 hours. Aaron tossed and turned the night before and he decided to get up early and get ready. He brushed his teeth, and picked out his clothes. He chose a light blue t-shirt with a small green lizard on the front. There were no words on the front of the t-shirt and the back had no picture or words. He considered this t-shirt his favorite out of all his t-shirts. He was going to wear a collared shirt but he didn't want to seem so formally dressed just to make cupcakes. Plus, he didn't want anyone thinking he was trying to overly impress her parents but he hoped they liked him. He chose black pair of shorts and some flapjacks sandals with no socks. He thought he looked cool but not over doing it. Although he had picked out his clothes the previous hour, out of respect for his family, he waited a bit before he showered. As he waited to shower, he looked at the purchased items once more to make sure everything was there. He went through all the paint and art supplies. He hoped he had enough of the paint colors, brushes and the paper. For the project, they had to make something and then draw and paint it and he figured there would be some attempts before they settled upon one that didn't have any mistakes or at least one they both liked. As the next hour came, he left the supplies in the bag and headed to the shower. His shower was quick as he had already brushed his teeth and he quickly got dressed. He was literally waiting for the sun to rise. He barely contained his excitement about the day. About 30 minutes later, he heard his mother stirring in the kitchen. He walked quickly in the kitchen not wanting to seem anxious but secretly hoping she was ready. NO! There she was in her robe 90 minutes before they had to be at Leyla's house. Aaron wondered how she could be so irresponsible and wasting time making coffee and not getting ready. Didn't she know they had to drive 12 minutes to Leyla's house? As he approached her, he gave her a small hug and even smaller smile, if any, and he gave her a quick "Mornin". He sat down at the kitchen table across from the chair where she had been sitting. She replied, "Good morning", surprised he was up so early. She was happy to see him, growing so fast and being a responsible young man but she did think he was up a little early for a Saturday morning. She remembered the conversation from last night and decided to focus on things that would help him relax. She wasn't a morning person nor was she going to pretend to be at this point. She needed coffee at this point to form clear, logical thoughts and as the smell of her coffee filled the room, she knew the pot of coffee she made was almost done or at least a cup had been made by now. She grabbed a cup from the cabinet above the coffee maker, poured some coffee in the cup and added some milk from the refrigerator. She returned to her chair across from Aaron who was watching her every move. He was still wondering why she wasn't ready, and he was hoping the coffee would help her move faster. NO! Here she comes to sit down AGAIN. He watched her pour the coffee and milk and his eyes drifted to her pink fluffy robe. He remembered when they bought it as a Mother's Day gift a few years ago. He remembered how much fun they had picking it out and wrapping it. The robe, which by now, was a few years old and his mom loved it and loved to wear it as evidenced by the wear and tear around the edges and collars. It had "Best Mom" embroidered on the left top side. As his mom sat down facing him with her hair pulled back into a pony tail, he waited to see how long it would take her to drink the steaming hot cup of coffee. She seemed to be savoring the moment as both her hands were cupped around the warm black mug. He was thinking what could he do to prompt her and she was thinking I am going to take my time and enjoy my coffee. As both faced each other trying to read each other body language and facial expressions, the silence would not be broken until Mary stumbled into the kitchen. "WHAT!" thought Aaron. "I'm hungry" Mary said. Aaron shot her a tough look, this was great, just what he needed- a half sleep mom, who was his ride to

Leyla's house, in her pink fluffy well-worn robe SLOWLY drinking hot coffee and now his little sister claiming she is hungry. Of all the mornings, why this morning. He didn't say anything rather he just watched this scene unfold. His sister had her favorite blanket around her shoulders and she plopped down in a chair beside Aaron. Well, he thought, "Get some food if you are so hungry but please don't ask mom to help you and you better not ask me". Inside, Aaron laughed at his thoughts. She started to yawn showing a few missing teeth. He thought she looked like cat sometimes when she yawned. "Trying to catch flies with that trap" he murmured towards his sister who now shot him back a tough look. His mother sensing a sibling fight about to happen decided to stop it before it started "What do you want Mary, I'll fix it for you". "NO!", thought Aaron, mom needs to get ready. "Mom, I'll help her so you can get ready" he said. His mom sort of surprised by his willingness to help his younger sister knew why he was so helpful. Since her coffee had woken her up a bit and she could form clear thoughts, she decided to have a little fun at Aaron's expense. "No, I'll fix her a nice big breakfast" mom said with a small smile. She saw Aaron's face cringe a little bit and she thought it was so funny. Aaron not quite sensing the humor his mother was attempting, decided to explain to his mother that his sister NEVER finishes her dinner or breakfast so a big breakfast wasn't a good idea. Her mom, still in a playful mood decided to counter him by saying his sister was growing and needed to eat. She couldn't continue so she burst out laughing while Mary watched this weird fight between mom and son over who would help her make breakfast. "Geesh" Mary said out loud, "I just want some cereal and I'll get it myself". She hadn't asked for help and she didn't have time for them to argue over it although she was enjoying seeing her brother squirming. She had a small laugh to herself about her thoughts yesterday "squirm cupcake boy, squirm". Aaron seeing her laughing, asked "What's so funny?" Mary didn't respond as she passed by him walking towards to the cabinet that had the cereal. Mom grabbed her coffee and was proceeding out the kitchen to get ready. "Finally", thought Aaron. After his mom left the room, he turned to Mary and said, "You better eat all of your food" as he walked to his room. He didn't see Mary stick her tongue out at him as he walked out.

Aaron had to be Leyla's house at 9am and it was 8:15 and his mom was STILL getting ready. "How long does it take" thought Aaron. He started to load the minivan with the supplies. He decided to wait outside and practice some of his swings with his tennis racket he had brought from his room. He practiced his backhand swings and moving to get into position for a backhand. After a few minutes, it was 8:30 and no mom. "Come on" he thought. At this precise moment was the reason why he wished he had his license and his own car. About 5 mins later, he could see her through the window moving inside the house as the door opened and her keys were jingling as she walked. He hopped in the minivan and put his racket in the backseat with the art supplies. As his mom backed out the driveway, he checked his watch, 8:40am. He hoped they wouldn't be late as he didn't want Leyla and her family to think he was a person who didn't respect their time, now if he could just get mom to press the gas harder and drive a little faster.

Leyla, being the host and a morning-type person, naturally was up early getting things ready, and setting things out. She got up, showered and decided to wear her tie-dyed t-shirt, a pair of jean shorts and some cute sandals she got last week. She wanted to be comfortable making the cupcakes. She straightened up the living room, putting pillows back on the couch neatly and putting things away. As she walked into the kitchen to double check the kitchen, she noticed a small figure walking into the living room and laying on the couch. This little figure was totally covered by a brown blanket with yellow, smiling dogs on it. She heard the heavy breathing under the blanket. She saw some toes sticking out one end of the blanket. "Oh Brother" she said. "Please don't let it be the brat who just so happen to wonder out to the living area next to the kitchen", she thought. "Seriously!" she said. Out of all the days he needed to wonder out here, it would be this Saturday morning. She still had over an hour before Aaron was due to arrive so she started thinking about the best way to handle this situation. She didn't think a sharp punch to the blanket was a bad idea, just not a good idea. "Bobby!", she shouted towards the blanket and gently nudged him. "What? Go away!" he replied back while his head was still covered by the blanket. She thought she had 2 choices: Do nothing and finish getting things ready OR drag him by his feet kicking and screaming all the way to his dirty room. She decided upon her first choice and to give him another few minutes, perhaps the noise from the kitchen would become so annoying that he would wake up and return to his room. Normally, she didn't mind or care about him sleeping the couch but since Aaron was coming over, she didn't want him to think they camped out and slept all over the house as a family. She returned to the kitchen and went through her checklist: cupcake pans, cupcake batter, utensils, cupcakes paper cups, decorations, ingredients to add to the cupcake batter and she had purchased some small dark blue aprons from the local store just for this occasion. She figured things may get messy while making the cupcakes and painting the pictures. As she finished her preparations, she started to wonder how would the scenario would play out. She started going through the flow of events as she imagined how they would happen. She thought-First, Aaron would arrive and her parents or she would answer the door. His parents would probably accompany him. They would walk in the house and her parents would smother them with small talk about the weather and this project. His parents would probably look around as her parents talked. Probably, after most of the small talk was almost over, his parents would be ready to go as things start to get awkward sitting or standing around. Just before his parents left, they would confirm a pick-up time with her parents and probably provide a number to call if they had problems. His parents would turn to leave, probably hug Aaron goodbye and remind him to be on his best behavior, which he would agree too. After Aaron parents would leave, Aaron would probably turn to Leyla and her parents....and....and......" What would happen next" she thought to herself. Would her parents continue to stay around offering to help them in the kitchen or worse sit and watch them from the living room or sit in the kitchen? To Leyla, the worse scenario would be having Bobby anywhere near the house while Aaron was there. She could escort her parents out or shoo them away but Bobby would cause tremendous embarrassment. Fortunately, he had a soccer game a little later in the morning so he would be gone and so would at least 1 parent. She didn't mind her parents being there, she just didn't want them to embarrass her in front of Aaron. She was disturbed from her thoughts as she heard small feet smacking against the kitchen tile floor. It was Bobby, the brat, looking for food. "I'm hungry" he said with the blanket over head so you could only see his eyes and nose only. He stopped near Leyla and waited. "What was he waiting for" she thought. Her patience was starting to wear thin even from this short encounter. "Hurry up and whatever you do, don't make a mess." she snapped at him. He shot her a look, half ignoring her from underneath the blanket. He just wanted her to move so he could get by and get to the kitchen table to drop off his blanket. He decided he wanted waffles and the only thing or person standing in between him and his waffles were Leyla. "Move" he snapped back. Apparently, he hadn't brushed his teeth yet because she could smell his morning breath. She slowly moved to the side so he could pass but she kept a close eye on him. He got his waffles and syrup and a glass of milk. He was watching her as he ate slowly. He was trying to think what the big deal was as it was only cupcakes. They could have bought some and saved the time. "Who was going to know" he thought but Little Miss Perfect wanted to do everything right and follow all the rules even though no one would know or was watching. He finished eating and simply got up, grabbed his blanket and walked out without saying anything and leaving his dirty plate, fork and glass on the table. "Oh Great!" Leyla said when she turned to see him walking out of the kitchen. As she was finishing washing her dishes and Bobby's dishes, her mom entered the kitchen in her powder blue robe. "Mom! You aren't going to be wearing that when Aaron's family arrives, are you?" she said to her mom, who seemed genuinely shocked at the tone. "I'm sorry, no good morning, no how are you" her mom replied sarcastically. She totally understood what her daughter was thinking and feeling. She recalled distinctly how it felt to have friends come over and how you want EVERYTHING to be perfect, especially if the guest was a boy. Her mom figured she had time to eat, get some coffee and get ready in plenty of time. She figured they were not the ones traveling so they had some time as the host. Plus, it was her dad that was still sleeping that she should be worried about not her. The two of them paused briefly and shared a sweet, knowing smile as her mom proceeded to make some instant coffee. She figured she would be quick about it to prevent any harsher stares or comments from Leyla. "Do you need help with anything" her mom asked, recalling the conversation from the previous night. Her mom went on, "Do you need help making the cupcakes". "No!"

Leyla said without hesitation and it came out a little snappy. She could see her mom jump a little, so she said in a calmer tone "Mom, I got it but thank you for offering". Leyla wanted to be nicer to her but she was afraid that her mom wouldn't change out of the comfortable robe she was wearing and get ready quickly. Very little was said afterwards and her mom finished making her coffee and stated sipping the steaming hot liquid. She took it back to her bedroom hoping this would help Leyla to relax. It did help Leyla to relax for about one second. Leyla finished her preparations and by 8:45am, everyone was up, dressed, fed and about the house either watching tv or in their rooms.

Everything appears scattered and in pieces until you put it all together- James Williams

As the minivan carrying Aaron and his mom turned right on Pear Street, they started looking for the 602 address on the mailbox. GPS was saying that 602 North Pear Street was up ahead on the right. Sure enough, there it was sitting there looking majestic. It was a single-story house with a large oak tree in the front yard with low branches perfect for climbing or hanging on. There was a family swing big enough for 3 or 4 small kids or 2 or 3 medium sized adults in the front of the house near the oak tree. The house was made of red brick with the driveway and garage towards the right side of the house. The lawn was maintained and neatly trimmed. There was a dark brown privacy fence that ran from both sides of the house and Aaron wondered how the backyard looked, was it as neat and well maintained as the front yard. The front yard was absent bikes, toys and showed no signs of wear or tear. He quickly wondered how often they played in the front yard probably not too often. His mother slowed the mini-van down to a stop very close behind the silver car parked outside the garage. He hoped she wouldn't accidently bump their car and start the morning off wrong. He checked his watch and it was 8:55am. "Perfect" he thought. As Aaron and his mother started to get out of the mini-van, the front door of the house opened with 4 smiling faces coming out of the front door. Aaron grabbed the supplies from the mini-van leaving his tennis racket in the back on the floor. Everyone introduced themselves to each other. Aaron's mother, Vanna, was the first to say something awkward, and it happened when she met Leyla. She said, "Oh you are Leyla, I've heard so much about you". Everyone laughed at the comment except Aaron who felt genuinely embarrassed and hope that no one would ask what she had heard or what did he say. Mike and Pam introduced themselves as Leyla's parents. The last one to meet Aaron was Bobby, who seemed mildly impressed by Aaron. Bobby could imagine Aaron as a cool big brother. He shook hands with Aaron the best he could. "So, let's go inside" Leyla's mom, Pam, said out loud. Aaron was thinking, "Everyone but my mother, please". Leyla grabbed the supplies from Aaron as the entered the house and took them to the kitchen briefly inspecting them. He and Leyla secretly knew this encounter of the parents would happen but what they didn't know was how long it would take. Torture to a 9th grader is meeting the parents of someone from school and having them engage in a lively conversation divulging all the family secrets like

31

how you were as a baby or some of your secret fears like crickets. "Please no baby stories", Aaron and Leyla both thought. As they went inside, the living room was large and open with dark brown, warm colors like the chocolate color couch and love seat. The pictures on the wall seemed to standout against the dark colors. Leyla forgot about the baby pictures on the wall, and the worst of all, the pictures of her with her front teeth missing. Leyla wished she could pause the world at this very moment, remove the pictures, and then restart the world. Aaron, seeing her clearly embarrassed, decided to help her out by not looking so much at the pictures and he turned to her and said, "I understand" and smiled. He knew if they were at his home, he would have to endure the same situation. As his mom looked around and Leyla's mom seemed determined to give a house tour, and play tour guide, Leyla decided to do something before they left the living room and go anywhere near her bedroom. Even though it was clean, the very thought of ANYONE from school seeing her room made her cringe. Leyla thought quickly and said, "How about we sit down, would you like something to drink?" Vanna replied, "No thank you". Aaron sensing Leyla needed help to avoid anything embarrassing tried to help again. He was hoping she was taking note of his assertive assistance. "I'll take a drink" he said. Everyone paused to listen to what he wanted. With all the attention on him so suddenly, Aaron seemed surprised by the attention, and stammered slightly, "I'll...I'll take some juice". He waited for Leyla to move but she stared back at him waiting along with the others. Pam, Leyla's mom, chimed in "What kind dear, orange, apple, which one?" "So many choices" thought Aaron. To Aaron, it was odd to have so many juices in a refrigerator. Aaron really wanted everyone to leave them alone and now he found himself between orange juice with pulp and apple juice. "I'll take apple juice" he said. Everyone sat down together like it was prearranged with the families sitting across from each other. Leyla's parents and brother sat on the same couch directly across Aaron and his mother who sat on the love seat. Awkward silence seemed to engulf the room as everyone started to wonder "What next?" Leyla returned with the juice for Aaron, "thank you" he said and awkwardly took the cup. Leyla sat down on the same couch as her family. Leyla's parents begin to wonder things like "I wonder how long she is going to stay, what else do I say and if I say something or if I share more will the conversation keep going and going". They too had things to do. Vanna, Aaron's mom, was wondering things like "Nice people, I really should be going, I got shopping to do, how long do I have to stay to be polite". With all these thoughts and everyone new to this type of situation, they all started talking at the same time. It was so funny that Bobby started to laugh at the adults while Leyla and Aaron watched this goofy scene. Bobby quickly stopped when he was sent a tough look by his dad. Small talk continued for another 10 minutes as they discussed what Leyla and Aaron would be doing. Then it dawned on all of them that Leyla and Aaron needed to start working on the project. Vanna was the first one to realize this and said "Well, let me go so they can get started". Everyone agreed, and she shook hands with everyone, hugged and kissed Aaron, much to his embarrassment and she was escorted to the door and left. Aaron was glad that his sister, Mary, didn't come and couldn't come because she was not dressed and ready when they left. Although Mary would have happily traveled in her pajamas, her mother refused to let her come dressed that way. Leyla turned to Aaron with a look like "What now?" Leyla saved them and herself by saying, "Ok, we are going to the kitchen to get started". They left and went to the kitchen. Her parents turned on the tv and Bobby went to his room. When they were alone in the kitchen, they turned to each other and started to laugh at the whole situation and the living room scene. They laughed so hard and so long that Pam shouted out "You guys ok in there". Leyla responded, "Yes mom!".

Well, here they were together in the kitchen. This is what they had been waiting for all week long and time seemed to stop for just a second. "Let's get started" Leyla said. She gave Aaron a brief tour of the kitchen and gave him his small apron which he held up in the air by the sides as if he was inspecting it for holes. "Don't be silly, put it on" she said sensing he never had an apron on before. She giggled a little at him as he slowly put it on backwards and then pretending he didn't he didn't know how to tie it. She told him what the plan was for this morning. They were going to make cupcakes, decorate them and draw and paint them. Making the cupcakes seemed easy to Aaron. Mix the batter, pour them in the cup, and cook. Leyla decided to have Aaron do the mixing while she added things to the batter. Leyla read the directions on the box and turned the oven on to preheat it. Working in comfortable silence, Aaron asked "Do you know how to cook good?" Leyla thought the question was funny and poorly worded. She answered it in two parts "Yes, I know how to cook and Yes, it is pretty good". Aaron never noticed the poorly worded question and proceeded "So, what is your favorite meal to make?" Leyla wondered why he was so focused on her cooking. She decided it didn't matter, they were working well together. She answered him "Mac and cheese, do you know how to cook?". Aaron decided to have fun with the answer. "Of course, I can cook anything" and he casually laughed. She knew he was joking. "What is your favorite meal to make" she played on. "Waffles in a toaster" he laughed as he said it. The two worked so well together, the cupcakes mixture was whipped up pretty good and Leyla complimented Aaron on his stirring skills and Aaron complimented her on her adding things to the mixture skills. In a short time, the cupcakes were being poured into the cups. Some of the batter spilled on the cupcake pan as Leyla poured. Aaron, being the good little helper he thought he was, and wanting to do his part, would wipe any spilled batter gently with a napkin. Soon, the cupcakes were ready for the oven. "Done" exclaimed Leyla, "Let's get them in the oven ". Carefully, tray after tray of cupcakes, Aaron handed the cupcake tray to Leyla and she carefully grabbed the cupcake pan and very slowly lowered them into the oven. Both were thinking that they were a good team. After the last pan was in the oven, Leyla stepped slowly back from the oven and lifted the oven door to close it.

As they waited in the kitchen, they continued to talk but the conversation turned sincerer. Leyla felt so comfortable and relaxed around him. They talked about their feelings about school, chess, friends, sports and how they felt about the project. He seemed like the type of guy who would call her just to say "Hi" and to say, "He was thinking about her". He listened as she explained how she got into chess. Her dad was a chess player and introduced it to her and she fell in love with the game and the time she spent with her dad. She felt that it helped her with her school work as well. Aaron listened intently as she spoke and wondered about her relationship with her family. They seem like they were good people, nothing weird about them but he knew every family had their unique ways but that wasn't his focus as he concentrated on what Leyla saying. Aaron had never played chess, primarily because he didn't have time. Plus, he like checkers better because the pace of play was faster. He loved watching her eyes light up as she talked about something she loved and how she spoke so passionately about her interests. He could tell that she was the type of person that devoted all of herself to something and it made him wonder if they were to date, would her eyes light up and she would speak so well about him. He directed his thoughts back to her and what she was talking about which was having a timer in chess. The oven timer sounded and broke into their interesting conversation. "Almost half way there", Aaron said meaning now that the cupcakes were done, now they could decorate, draw and paint them. "Wow, they look and smell good" Leyla exclaimed loudly. She said it so loud that Bobby heard it from his room and he took that as his queue to investigate the sweet smell of cupcakes. He came bouncing into the kitchen with a big smile on his face. He saw Aaron and Leyla looking over and inspecting the cupcakes. He thought Aaron was tall and wondered if Aaron would play soccer with him or if Aaron thought he was cool. Bobby wanted to appear cool in front of Aaron so he thought he would try a less aggressive strategy to get a cupcake, "Do you guys need any help" he asked excitedly. "NO!" Layla shot back. "Well, can I watch?" he asked and the response was the same just louder followed by "MOM! Bobby is in the kitchen disturbing us". Her mom asked Bobby to leave and to get ready because he had a soccer game in about an hour. "No cool points lost there", Bobby thought as he put his head down, and left the kitchen hoping that he would be able to take and eat one of the cupcakes before the soccer game.

The sweet smell of cupcakes filled the house and Leyla's dad, Mike, came wondering in after Bobby. "Is it time to taste them yet?" he asked playfully. Leyla, getting perturbed by the family interruptions, gave him "the look". She was thinking if it wasn't Bobby then it was dad. She was afraid that dad's presence would cause her mom to come into the kitchen. If her parents came into the kitchen, Leyla felt it would totally change the vibe and her parents would go into parent over drive. She had to prevent it from getting to that point. "Dad, remember Bobby's soccer game", she quickly replied. "Oh, that's right" he said, "I need to get ready and get Bobby ready, thanks for reminding me". He left the kitchen calling for Bobby to get ready. "It worked", Leyla happily thought. Bobby and Mike left shortly afterwards and they said "bye" to everyone. Bobby pleaded again for a cupcake before he left but no luck. Finally, Leyla and Aaron were alone again. Selecting the cupcakes, as a project, seemed like a good idea a few weeks ago but now they had a batch of piping hot cupcakes in front of them. Silently, they thought at the same time, "Now what" because they were too hot to decorate. They decided to talk outside and sit on the swing while the cupcakes cooled down. "Oh yes, the swing" thought Aaron, he recalled seeing it when he arrived at her house. They didn't want to sit in the living with her mom and watch tv and they were not allowed in Leyla's room so outside seemed the best place since the kitchen was hot from the baking. When they went outside, they were greeted with a slight breeze and warm sunshine. The weather seemed to agree with them being outside and with the angle of the sun, the large oak tree casted a beautiful shadow and shade over the swing. Aaron let her sit down first on the right side and he sat on the left side. At first, they said nothing as they watched the lite traffic go by and the neighbors either working in the yards. They watched them cut the grass in silence and trim the small bushes. It was like they were watching a movie and neither wanted to talk. As awkward as teenagers are, these two seemed totally at peace and at ease with each other. So much at peace that they forgot about the cupcakes as they finally started to talk and talk and talk. 5 mins turned to 20 mins and after about 30 mins outside sitting, watching and talking, Leyla's mom came to the door "Ummm, are the cupcakes out here now" she laughed. She was watching them from the window, although she trusted them, and she thought they made a "cute couple". She knew Leyla and Aaron would hate it if she said that to them. Aaron and Leyla returned to the cupcakes and a lot of questions like how to decorate them and how many to decorate and use in the picture and everything else. It seemed funny as they stood there looking at a dozen or so of cupcakes. Aaron was the one that thought they should keep it simple and not over complicate things. His idea was to take 2 cupcakes each and she would decorate 2 and he would decorate 2 cupcakes with happy faces. They laughed again at the thought. The rest of the cupcakes they could decorate divide up and eat. Aaron was more worried about the drawing and painting. He was hoping they could finish it today but realistically he wasn't sure. It was almost lunch time and he was getting hungry. He figured if they did the first part of baking and decorating, perhaps after lunch they could work on the drawing and painting. He mentioned this to Leyla and she agreed to keep it simple and the 2 cupcakes was a good idea. She liked how they discussed things, worked together in making decisions and moved forward with the plan. She didn't like it when people had no ideas and criticized your ideas or they had an idea and they were unwilling to be flexible but to her Aaron wasn't like that. He had his own ideas and listened to her ideas and offered creative suggestions. This was also noticed by her mom who was secretly listening from the living room but she could only pick up bits and pieces of the conversation but she found their personalities worked well together.

The cupcake decorating went very well. Aaron and Leyla acted so silly painting all the cupcakes and picking out the 2 out they wanted. They had so much fun together decorating the cupcakes. After they finished decorating the cupcakes, Aaron suggested Leyla arrange them how she wanted. She basically put them in a line and made sure all the cupcakes were facing the same direction. "Simple yet perfect" Aaron thought. They took pictures of the cupcakes in case they were not able to finish everything. "Happy Cakes are here again" Aaron said and they burst out laughing.

After the decorating, Leyla and Aaron decided to eat lunch first and then work on the drawing and painting of the cupcakes. Leyla's mom made some sandwiches for all of them and they decided to eat some of the extra cupcakes for dessert. At the kitchen table, all 3 of them sat around the table eating and talking. Pam asked Aaron many questions about his family, tennis and school which he answered confidently and clearly. Leyla thought she was being a little nosey but glad she asked because she liked how Aaron handled himself while her mom interrogated him. He was cool and calm under the questioning. Aaron talked about his parents, Robert and Vanna, and his little sister, Mary. Leyla thought his little sister sounded a lot like her little brother Bobby and Aaron agreed. He told them how he got into tennis and that his parents were tennis players. His life and family seemed very interesting to Pam but she didn't want to pry too much and make him uncomfortable. The conversation flowed very naturally with all of them, they laughed, joked and the conversation flowed well beyond lunch time. Leyla didn't want their lunch together to end rather she wanted her mom to go back to the living room or her room so she could spend time with Aaron again without anyone else there. She admitted to herself that she was starting to "like" him. Everyone cleaned up and Leyla wiped the table down. After wiping down the table, Leyla put down an old table cloth to protect the table. She found the bag of art supplies and begin taking them out and putting them on the table. After a few minutes of discussing the plan, Leyla would get things started. Leyla, being slightly more artistic than Aaron, drew the outlines on the canvass paper that Aaron had brought. Afterwards, they started painting the drawings but they soon realized that two people painting on the same canvass at the same time is not easy BUT FUN. They would accidently bump the other person's arm when they are painting. This happened so often they had to use 2 or 3 more canvass papers because the mistakes could not be corrected. They finally finished and the painting looked pretty good. They thought they did a great job and so did Leyla's mother. They signed their names on the front of the canvass like real artists and they put the painting to the side to let it dry. They took pictures of the finished product, the final version of the painted canvass of cupcakes.

It was nearly 4'oclock when Aaron looked at his watch, "What a great day" thought Aaron. They had pretty much finished around the time they thought they would and Aaron knew his mother be there around 4:30pm. Instead of calling her to pick him up early and stress her, Leyla and Aaron decided to go back outside to the swing. By this time, the shadow from this morning had moved from the swing and they were in the sunshine and the slight breeze was still there. After they sat down and started talking, Aaron started asking her questions. His first question was if she could be anything, what would it be? She thought about for a few seconds and slowly responded, "A flower, a beautiful flower that once planted, bloomed in the spring and lived forever". "Wow" Aaron said as he was surprised about how passionate she was about flowers. He noticed some in a vase in her living room and she had a rose saved as the screensaver on her cellphone. "Obviously", Aaron thought, "she loves flowers". Aaron made a mental note to himself about this detail. Continuing, Aaron asked her what kind of movies she liked and disliked. She liked comedies but not horror movies. He waited and then slowly and confidently asked "Did you want to go to the movies sometime?". Leyla, a little surprised, wanted to confirm what she thought she heard. "Are you asking me out?", she asked. Aaron laughed at her question and reminded her not to answer a question with a question. Leyla, not wanting to send him the wrong message that she wasn't interested, quickly replied with a smile "Sure, when?" She hoped she didn't appear desperate or too eager. Deep down inside, both were so excited and happy at the thought of them going on a date. Although he asked and she said "sure" both were unsure about what their parents would say about it.

They were not allowed to go on dates just yet. As they sat there in silence thinking about this, they decided to be honest and discuss this with their parents. They would tell them that it wasn't a date, which was true, and they were friends hanging out catching a movie together, which was also true. It is also true that catching a movie and hanging out is the same thing people do when they go on dates. Oh well, they decided to bring it up and be honest with their parents, it was a date. There was no rush to go, they would see if they could go next weekend. Just as they finished up the conversation, Aaron's mom was slowly pulling into the driveway, late by 15 perfect minutes, thought Aaron. He had a big smile on his face as she stopped the car but his smile quickly faded as he saw Mary in the backseat.

*The good news is we are going in the same direction,
the great news is that we will arrive at the same
destination-* James Williams

In the week and weeks that passed, Leyla and Aaron
turned in their art project and got an A for creativity,
teamwork and overall presentation. Also, Leyla and
Aaron's parents agreed to let them date after they all
met at Aaron's house to discuss them going out. It
seemed so formal for the two teens to have the two
families meet but it was a great meeting for both
families and their siblings didn't embarrass them too
much. The siblings got along well much to everyone's
suprise. Leyla and Aarons' relationship flourished in the
weeks and months that followed. They talked nearly
every day on the phone and on the weekends, they
usually had something planned either together or with
the families as part of the dating arrangement. The
picture, they took of the Happy Cakes cupcakes, was
printed on larger paper, and two copies were made,

one for Aaron and one for Leyla. The pictures were in color, and hug on each other's bedroom wall. This picture would serve as a reminder of not only the art project but also when they really got to know each other in a special, unique way. It would be a mark in time when they worked side by side as a team, two true leaders, true teamwork and collaboration, 2 minds working together on one concept, one project, each giving, sharing and contributing to the common goal. This picture would represent the beginning of their relationship and remind them relationships take teamwork. For teenagers, the picture was important because of the way teenagers' express feelings and emotions. For teenagers, their relationships and the way they express love is different. For example, one must understand teenage relationships and the word love. Teenagers typically don't use the word love not because they don't believe in it rather, they see love in different categories. First, family love is the first way a teenager sees love and experience love as it is their first love experience. Love is shown to them and they hear it from their parents so they will tell a mom or dad that they love them because they understand family love. This family love dominates the love in the teenagers' life and love circle. Out of a teenager's 100% love circle in their life, this is 50% of their love circle. For many of the teenagers, love is expressed and known as family love. 25% of the remaining 50% in a teenager's love circle is reserved for things they love like cheeseburgers, close friends, French fries or the latest gadget or style. There is no fear or shame in the teenagers to express love for anything in this category. So, 75% of the 100% teenager love circle consists of family love, close friends, food or things and they aren't afraid to say it. However, the remaining 25% is typically applied to the boyfriend or girlfriend or personal relationships. Typically, they don't say "I love you" to them and typically because this love is different from the other categories in the teenager's love circle. With the other love categories, it is shown, demonstrated and they reciprocate it. With the last 25% in their love circle, it is literally uncharted territory. The only way to experience it is to experience it and there are traditional social or cultural aspects that can override the expressing of that emotion. For example, take a teenage boy. For a boy in love, most of the time, he will not say "I love you" to girl in front of others because he doesn't want to be seen as weak or sappy, so he may never say it to his girlfriend in public, around his friends and rarely if ever in private except mumbled in a response to her when she says she loves him. So, for a teenage boy, the 25% reserved for this category, is rarely fully experienced. They experience like 1% out of the 25% meaning they don't get to experience it and to benefit from it fully. For example, saying "I love you" to his girlfriend, he will only say it, if ever, 1% of the time and it is usually mumbled. Most of the time, a teenage boy never says, "I love you" except to family. For a teenage girl, it is very similar, her 25% is like 1% as well, the differences are when and why she says I love you. She is hesitant to say, "I love you" to a boy because she is afraid he may not say it back and she is left hanging emotionally. She is afraid it may make her seem desperate and clingy. Well, her concerns are somewhat validated because in most cases upon hearing a girl tell her boyfriend that she loves him, it makes him feel soft inside and he is trying to imagine the next steps in the relationship. He is probably thinking "Now I have to spend all my time with you, can't hang with my friends, and I have to buy presents, call you all the time and feel like I can't do anything by myself anymore." This can be suffocating to teenage boy. Although love is supposed to liberating, to a teenage boy, hearing a girl tell him that she loves them, the teenage boy thinks and feels his freedom is curtailed. The teenage girl wants to say it but doesn't so her 25% is reduced to 1% and thus she isn't able to fully experience it fully. The teenage girls aren't able to fully experience the 25%, meaning to say, "I love you", and to hear it said back to them thus feeling love is being reciprocated. So, for teens, boys or girls, their 25% is reduced to 1%. The 24% isn't lost, rather it is developed as they get older and as they experience more personal relationships. By the time they grow up and get married and have kids, their love circle is at 100% and they are fully experiencing love. It is only as a teen that they can't fully experience love and say it. Leyla and Aaron were starting to experience part of the 24% much sooner than anyone expected, especially themselves, and much sooner than most teens or adult experience in life.

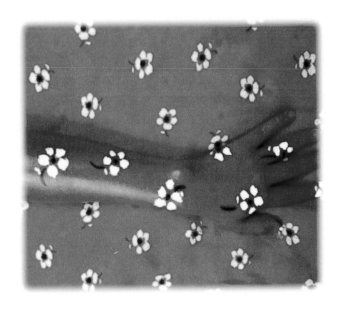

The closer we become, the more we become as one and we are seen as one- James Williams

For Leyla, she was trying to imagine life before Aaron and why hadn't they talked like this before in their previous grades together. She thought about the times she saw him previously at school and other events and perhaps the opportunity didn't present itself. People often wonder about this but they forget they were probably in a different place in their life, and their maturity level may have been different. Honestly, to Leyla, Aaron was the best of both worlds. He was tough but he was kind. He was mature but he was silly at times. He was a nice guy, even though some guys hate hearing it, but he was confident with a slight attitude. She figured that playing tennis helped to shape his personality and maturity. She had watched tennis on tv but didn't find it too interesting until she met Aaron. Now, she had attended at least one of his tournaments although he didn't seem to do well when she was there. She noticed that tennis, like chess, it is just you against your opponent. So, you had to believe in yourself, problem solve for yourself and compete. She thought tennis was part of reason he was so confident. Also, she noticed that tennis had the high level of sportsmanship, just like chess. He was a good communicator in the fact that he listened to her, and thought before he spoke. He wasn't trying to take from her and pressure her into doing something she didn't want to do or to be someone that she wasn't, he let her be herself. And, while being herself, she found herself and a new relaxed and confident Leyla with Aaron. His confidence made her more confident. His ability to listen made her a better communicator. His consistency made her aware of changes in her personality, behavior and overall attitude towards things. She was becoming a better person because of Aaron. His gentlemen ways reminded her that she was a young lady, not a girl and the fact that he took her serious, made her mature in other parts of her life, like the encounters with her parents. Her parents noticed this in her and it made them smile inside. Privately, her parents talked about how Aaron was a good young man and they were happy he was having a positive impact upon Leyla from that perspective. They had heard from other parents that when their teenage daughter meets a guy who is negative and has a bad influence on their daughter, it can lead to other problems or issues. As Leyla sat in her room, she wondered how she would have been without Aaron and where would she be without Aaron. Would she be watching tv and eating chips or hanging out with her friends from the chess club? She didn't know because she couldn't imagine life without him just as she couldn't imagine life before him. As she sat thinking about it, she silently thanked Aaron for making her a better person without even trying and without her knowing...."that's magical", she thought.

For Aaron, he was starting to really feel emotions for Leyla that he hadn't really experienced before, and he really liked her. Her presence interfered with time and his brain. For example, she made the days without him seeing her seem long yet the time they spent together seemed short. She made the food they ate together taste better but she makes him not recall what they ate. She made him genuinely smile inside when he was around her but he didn't feel like smiling when she wasn't around-he missed her. The impact she was having upon him was immense, so intense that he felt he wanted to write a poem for her. He had never written a poem for anyone before, not even his mother on Mother's Day but for Leyla, he felt compelled to really tap into what little artistic side he had and try to impress her and express himself. She was worth the awkward effort no matter how corny it may sound to anyone, he really felt that Layla deserved to have something from his....his....dare he say heart and soul. He laughed as he thought about it but he wanted her to know. He learned from his mother that small things mean a lot to some girls. For example, the poem may be poorly written BUT the fact that he took the time to write it made it mean more. His mother always mentioned to him that for some girls, small things are a big deal. For example, remembering the day you met, how you met, and the details of the discussion when you met would mean a lot more than buying a card, and writing your name at the bottom or buying some expensive gift. It was truly the thought that counted and to know that someone was thinking about you. Plus, Aaron wasn't working, buying an expensive gift was out of the question he laughed and plus, Leyla didn't seem like she was a materialistic type of person. She wasn't fussy about clothes or shoes. If flowers were what she loved, then he would write a poem about flowers and he would surprise her. He started working on it each day and it was stressing him a bit because it was really outside his comfort zone and he wasn't totally focusing on his studies or tennis practice. He started thinking this was probably better for someone who had more of an artistic mind, his mind was very logical. He thought about Leyla and he thought about his mother's words so he pressed forward with his poem. He just kept imagining himself presenting it to her and how happy and surprised she would be.

His best effort for a hand-drawn picture and poem about a flower for Leyla yielded this....

A FLOWER FOR THE LADY

As the sun rises in the east
And sets in the west
There is something in my head
I want to get off of my chest
If I tell her how I feel
I'm not sure what she would say
Maybe I can show her my love
By giving her this bouquet

A flower for the Lady
Would brighten up her day
It would show how much I care
And the words I could not say

Giving these flowers to her
So that she will know
That like the flowers with proper care
our love will grow.
I pray to God above
That she will know how I feel
That the love I have in my heart
Is so very real.
A flower for the lady because she is worth it
A flower for the lady because she deserves it.

"Corny right?" he thought. He didn't feel comfortable
using the word love in the poem but he had no choice.
What other word could he use? Love, as a word, is
irreplaceable. Love, as an emotion, is sincere. Love, as
a life, is fulfilling. He couldn't think of any word to
replace love and he really cared about her. He hoped it
didn't make her feel as awkward as he felt. He also
used the word God. In his faith, he believed in God and
he knew Leyla and her family believed in the same God
because she briefly mentioned it during their many
nights on the phone. Although they never had an in-
depth conversation about it, he knew they shared the
same faith. Again, what other word could he use? God
was irreplaceable to him and in his poem. He didn't
want the poem to be heavy but creativity knows no
limits and he didn't want to create a half sincere
sounding poem. If that was the case, then he would
just write on a piece of paper "I saw a flower and
thought of you". Simple, yet….yet…..too simple for
what he was feeling about Leyla. Poem finished, hand-

written, he double checked the spelling, and he would present it to her at their next date at the mall for all the world to see him doing something outside his teenager comfort zone. For a moment, doubt crept into his mind and he began to worry that at the mall, Leyla would laugh at him very loud, so loud that people would stop to check on her. In the process of checking on her, they would ask what caused the big laughter and she would be compelled to respond to them. She was say "the poem Aaron wrote" and they would ask to look at it...and she would be nice and show it to them since they stopped to help her....they would read it, and think "corny, right?".....then they too would break out into a big laughter...."not good" thought Aaron. He quickly dismissed that scenario and he prayed that it wouldn't happen. Saturday evening, they were going to meet at the mall to watch a movie, and he would present it to her there before the movies, he couldn't wait to see her and her response to the poem.

Love is illusive and can slip away easily so everyone is trying to tackle it as capturing love is the only way you score- James Williams

On Saturday, Leyla and Aaron met outside the local mall about 2 hours before the movie started around noon. Aaron was dropped off first and a few minutes later, Leyla's mom dropped her off near the same front entrance. As they were coming around the curve, Leyla saw Aaron standing there and instantly smiled when she saw him. As she got out of the car, she told her mom, "I love you" as she closed the door. She was still had a big smile on her face as she approached Aaron, who was now smiling as he saw her pull up and get out of the car. Aaron was watching anxiously for her because today he was going to present the poem to her. He paced a little as he waited. He knew that he couldn't miss her because the mall traffic, near that entrance, was one-way traffic so he was watching very intently for her from that direction. Now that she was here, he was so happy. After a brief hug, they went to the movie theatre, and Aaron purchased the movie tickets with the money his dad given him. Having so much time before the movie started, Aaron and Leyla decided to hang out in the food court area and maybe get something to drink and eat. Aaron had brought the poem and it felt very heavy and hot like it was a small ball of fire. He laughed as he thought the poem might burn a hole in his left breast shirt pocket. As they entered the food court area, it was crowded with all the local high school kids, and families with small kids running around. Aaron sarcastically thought "This is going to be great" and he was starting to get a little nervous. Everyone prepares for these moments differently but when the moment arrives, that when you are truly tested. Leyla sensed Aaron was a bit uneasy but she didn't know what was bothering him. She figured she would inquire once they sat down. They got 2 bottles of water and no food for now because both ate before they left their houses. They found a place to sit that was sandwiched between a lady and her oversized stroller with a kid inside and toddler stumbling around. On the other side was an elderly couple that appeared to be watching every move they made as they ate their food. Aaron hoped that the kids, on the left side, didn't come to their table and disturb them and he hoped the elderly couple, on the right side, didn't start asking questions or offer any advice once he got started. As they opened their water bottles, and started to sip the water, Aaron asked Leyla "How was your day?" She told him that she basically got ready and ran a few errands with her mother. Aaron appeared to be listening but Leyla kept noticing he wasn't calm and at ease like he is normally. She decided to ask him "Are you ok? You seem nervous or anxious". Aaron tried to laugh it off "I'm fine but there is something I want to share with you". Leyla appeared to be surprised. Aaron tried to tell her that he really cared about her and enjoyed spending time with her. She nodded and listened with a small smile. "I wrote something for you" Aaron said and paused for the earth to stop shaking underneath his feet. "What?" Leyla said slowly. Aaron fumbled in his pocket and pulled out a piece of paper. She wondered how he kept it so neat without wrinkling it too much. Also, she was surprised at how he seemed a little nervous, which wasn't like him. He told her he had wrote something for her, a poem. She slowly put her hands to her mouth and slightly gasped which made Aaron just a little bit more nervous. After calming his nerves, he told her that he really cared about her and presented the poem to her as onlookers, consisting of the two groups on the opposite end of the age spectrum, young and old, watched as if they were designated witnesses. Other onlookers included were people passing by and seeing a girl with her hand cupped to her mouth and boy who seemed nervous. They drew attention in the busy, noisy mall and at this point, Aaron didn't care and his confidence was restored as Leyla slowly took the paper while looking into Aaron's eyes. She slowly read the poem as Aaron watched her eyes go line by line. "Aaron", she said with emotions building up inside her....."Thank you, I love it" she said and reached to hug him tightly. He was so happy and his heart was filled with so much joy, he could just have walked out of the mall with Leyla right now. He wondered how a movie could top this moment. They talked about the poem and his use of the words in the poem. Aaron explained the best he could as he tried to cherish the moment and cherish Leyla. Leyla was surprised as no one had ever given her a poem and the fact that he took the time to write it made it more special. And, as if that wasn't enough, he wrote it about one of the things she was most passionate about, flowers, and he drew a very nice picture of flowers. She was genuinely impressed. As they sat staring and smiling at each other, they eventually started talking again. After another 30 minutes, they decided to get something to eat before the movie. They couldn't stop thinking about the moment, this day, the poem, and their relationship...This was probably the best day of their young lives....

Besides everything, what else is wrong with this picture?- James Williams

About two months into the relationship and about 5 months after school started, they realized that it was almost Christmas. While everything was going so well, there were somethings that were not going well. Aaron and Leyla had begun to shun the things they did before their relationship and they started to spend their free time with each other. For Leyla, she stopped attending the chess club as much as before citing very little time and her interest was waning. She still loved it but because of Aaron, she'd rather spend that time with him. For Aaron, the extra time he would spend practicing tennis, he was spending it with Leyla. His tennis game begun to be negatively impacted. He still loved the game but because of Leyla, he didn't practice with the focus and fervor he normally practiced and he started to lose against players he would normally beat. Leyla's chess club players begged her to come back and she tried but she was willing to sacrifice it to spend more time with Aaron. Some of her friends spoke to her privately about being so invested into one person and not doing things she enjoyed before. Leyla listened to her friends but they were not able to persuade her. She didn't tell all of them about the poem but the poem was powerful to Leyla and she felt really committed to Aaron. For Aaron, his tennis team knew that some players get burned out but they never thought Aaron would. He loved tennis and he was pretty good. To not have him at practice, it impacted the other players. When strong players compete against their teammates, it makes everyone better. In Aaron's absence, the team didn't have one of their leaders, one of their captains and one of their friends to push them and encourage them. The coaches mentioned this to Aaron and he understood what they were asking of him but Leyla seemed to make him happier than competing in a sport. In addition to neglecting their activities, friends and sport, both of Leyla and Aaron's grades begin to suffer. They were two honor roll students who were now making average or below average grades. When you aren't dating someone, you have a lot of free time to study, practice and do extracurricular activities. Once you start dating, the person you are dating tends to compete for that time and your attention. Leyla and Aaron didn't study like they did before they started dating and their grades begin to dip and they were turning things in late or not at all as evidenced by the latest report cards. Their parents were monitoring the situation for their child. Each of their parents had spoken to them about their grades and assignments and the teenagers promised to do better but the test grades and report cards didn't seem like they were successful at trying to do better. From their parents' perspective, they were not sure what to do. You had two teenagers that were great as a couple but their relationship was impacting their grades and school work as some projects were turned in late and they saw an increase in their tardiness to class as they would talk and walk to different classes together. The parents were stunned. Two good kids but their relationship wasn't helping them in school and they wondered what the impact it would have upon their future. Leyla's parents had thought she would either get a scholarship in chess or an academic scholarship. Aaron's parents thought he would get a scholarship in tennis or an academic scholarship. Their parents felt an overwhelming sense that their futures were being jeopardized and they felt the short-term gain of the relationship would lead to long term problems. They had witnessed some teens go down this path and not do well in school and college goals were no longer an option. To them, college was mandatory and the path to a decent life and lifestyle and this situation made them grieve for the future for not only their own child but the other child as well. Also, they worried about the impact this would have upon the respective siblings. If the siblings saw they were not making good grades, then they would wonder why the standard was different for them. As the parents continued to think about it, they started to question their decision to let them date and in some way, they felt it was their fault, but they couldn't have predicted that this would happen. No one can predict whether a relationship will work out or the impact it will have upon the people in the relationship or the families or their lifestyles. Sometimes, in bad relationships, only one person is affected but this relationship was different. In this relationship, the kids were good and the relationship wasn't negatively affecting them mentally, they were not being emotionally harmed, rather their grades, and future was going to be impacted if they continued with the relationship. No one exists as an island, they knew that this may impact their siblings. It had already started impacting their siblings at home. The parents were so focused on the teens that they were not giving attention to siblings who started having behavioral issues at home and in class. The parents felt like all their lives were spiraling out of control and they need to do something even though it was during the holidays. The parents secretly met shortly after Thanksgiving, first the moms and then both parents. They discussed the teens' relationship, the impact of the relationship honestly and in great detail. They didn't point fingers because they loved both kids and their families. They didn't feel like someone was to blame rather it was just how things were and they knew every relationship was different and unpredictable. As Aaron and Leyla continued to date as the parents secretly met on 3 separate occasions. Instead of a parents' date-night, the parents were secretly meeting with the other parents. The parents were not sure what would happen if the teens broke up. It could be devastating to the kids, families and siblings so they weren't sure what to do. Aaron's parents had already spoken with him and Leyla's parents had already spoke to her so the teens were aware but to them the relationship was making them feel so good inside and happy. During some of the discussions with their parents, Aaron and Leyla would ask their parents, "What is better; for me to be happy or my grades?" How do parents answer a question like that? Teens or kids don't think too much about the future as their experiences are extremely limited and parents tend to think about the kids' future more than the kids which is why parents try so hard to teach the kids how to behave, how to be mature and responsible and to take care of your life and your future. Leyla and Aaron were not disrespectful to their parents nor were they being defiant but they could only see their relationship, Aaron only saw Leyla and Leyla only saw Aaron.

At the last secret parents' meeting, the parents decided they would talk to the teens together and see what they would say when the issue was discussed all together face to face. They scheduled this meeting the first Saturday of Christmas break at Aaron's home. Leyla's family traveled in almost total silence on their way to Aaron's house. Her brother sensing a heavy mood, decided to just look out the window as he had heard discussions with Leyla and their parents about this issue. Upon arrival at Aaron's house, they were greeted by Aaron's dad. He offered them something to drink and they were all chatting lightly when Aaron's mom came out with Mary. Aaron's dad, Robert, said "Can we talk on the patio and let the littles ones watch tv?". The siblings were watching tv as both sets of parents, Leyla and Aaron went to the patio. Aaron and Leyla held hands as they sat on the patio couch across from their parents. Aaron's parents spoke first and then Leyla's parents. They spoke calmly and slowly highlighting the impact of the relationship upon their lives and potentially, their future. The teens listened respectfully to the parents and thought about what they were going to say. The moment was very tense and their mothers started to wipe their eyes as they imagined how the kids felt. The dads' eyes were watering as well. The teens started to slowly cry. Leyla first and at the sight of Leyla crying, Aaron started to cry like he has never cried before in front of anyone. Aaron spoke first while holding Leyla's hand, "Don't you want us to be happy?" he said through tears. Leyla thought he seemed so brave and courageous for speaking up for their relationship. She was proud of him even more. No one responded to Aaron's loaded question. There was no right answer in this situation. The silence engulfed the group and their stomachs churned. The siblings, inside watching silly cartoons, were totally unaware of how heavy and tense the situation was outside. Although it was a beautiful, crisp night, it could have been raining rocks and dirt to Leyla and Aaron. The parents had decided before the meeting that they were not going to make any suggestion of a breakup but the teens had to realize that this was serious to them. As the silence continued and the weeping continued, the parents were imagining how they would end this meeting tonight. Their parents hadn't thought about this or planned how to end the meeting or how would they close the meeting. Now, everyone sat on the patio, with the kids crying and staring at their parents, their hands locked together staring at their families' faces, staring at the people they loved and who loved them and they knew they cared about them but they also knew they cared about each other. "Now what" thought the parents and secretly they were upset they didn't have an exit plan to the meeting. Mike, Leyla's dad, broke the silence…." Please think about it" and he quickly followed, "I think it is getting late and we need to get going". The other parents agreed, everyone wiped their eyes as they entered the house where they kids were still watching the silly cartoons on tv….

When couples, once in love, break up; everyone sees the same thing differently like a shattered robot, an angry beaver, small rockets, steeple or a black box all in the same picture- James Williams

In the week that followed the meeting at Aaron's house with all the parents, there appeared to be a cooling down period with Aaron and Leyla's relationship meaning that Aaron and Leyla didn't call each other, and didn't hang out together. No one told them to do this rather they were numb and speechless. They were like teenage zombies. They were kids who didn't know what to do. They felt the same way without even saying anything to each other. Finally, on Saturday, one week after the meeting with the parents, Aaron decided to contact Leyla to talk about what happened the previous weekend. They agreed to meet at the local park with their parents' permission. They were on Christmas break and neither had any plans that weekend. They were honest with their parents that they were meeting to talk about the meeting they had with the parents. Their parents understood and allowed them to meet. The parents weren't sure what impact it would have upon the situation if they didn't let them meet. When Leyla and Aaron met at the park, they hugged tightly for a very long time. It was like they were clinging to each other for support and because their future together was uncertain. The discussion started out to catching up on things they had missed talking about during the week. Leyla and Aaron shared with each other that they hadn't done much during the week. They apologized to each other for not contacting each other. The conversation was going well until they reached the topic concerning the meeting with their parents. The question they kept asking themselves was "What do we do?" What is the correct answer to this question and what is the right answer to this question? As kids, as teenagers, they didn't know. Life doesn't prepare you for situations like this and if their parents didn't know what to do, how were they supposed to know what to do. This situation was causing them to grow up faster than anyone anticipated. Their relationship had evolved to this point and now they were deciding what to do and what were the next steps. As they looked at each other, they were thinking seriously about the situation they were experiencing. They very much respected their parents and they wanted to make their parents happy and they admitted to each other that they were not doing what they were supposed to be doing because of their relationship. It was almost like in love you lose a piece of yourself, that's part of the sacrifice that comes with love. In this case, they were losing in their educational life and other parts of their life. Therefore, their parents were worried that this sacrifice at such an early time in their life was going to set them up for failure later in life. Based upon the parents' experiences, they were trying to help the teenagers. It was if the past was talking to the present about the future. How could anyone know the future? In the present, their grades and other activities were negatively impacted. Was it more important for them to be happy now or later or could they have both? They had been thinking long and hard about this. Their grades mattered and their futures mattered and they were not taking this lightly. Considering their parents' feedback and the presentation of the facts at the meeting, Leyla and Aaron decided that they should break up for their own good now and for their futures.

Although they decided it, they were not sure it would work. Were they too deep in the relationship? If they broke up, would it guarantee their grades would get better? A broken heart, could be just as much of a distraction as their relationship, and a heart in love. There was no guarantee of nothing. There was no guarantee that if they stayed together that all the things they were trying to accomplish wouldn't be accomplished or it would be difficult to accomplish. This to them didn't seem fair that two good kids had to make such a tough decision so early in life with no guarantee of anything either way now or in the future. In life, love isn't a guarantee, a right but a privilege for those that find it in another person. There is no guarantee you are going find love at all or that you will grow up, fall deeply in love, get married and start a family....there is no guarantee at all. Love isn't guaranteed so if it isn't guaranteed, what was being guaranteed by them breaking up? What are you supposed to do if you meet a person and you think that you have found the illusive love but it is having a negative impact upon your life? They started to cry together at what they had just decided. They started to miss each other although the other person was sitting beside them. They wondered what their parents would say, would they be supportive or think they made the wrong decision. Would they applaud their maturity or would they think they were too quick to make the decision?

Also, they wondered if love was supposed to be selfish. The heart, which where love is kept, knows what it wants but if what it wants has a negative impact upon the person, should the heart to continue to want it or be allowed to have it? Although they wanted to remain together, would it be selfish of them to remain together despite the negative impact it was causing in their lives? Selfish, they were not, but at this moment, they wanted to be selfish even for only a moment. They may have found "the one" and they were letting "the one" get away. It made them think about how the heart is pure emotions and doesn't have a brain. Rather, the heart has a heart and that's it. It isn't designed to think logically that's why it has the mind to think and protect it. This was a clear case of heart versus mind and to make this decision, their hearts and minds were working together for their own good, like they were supposed too. However, if they completely disregarded the mind, then the heart would win and get what it wanted and their lives may suffer in the end as a result. If the mind gets what it wants without considering the heart's feelings, then meaningful, heartfelt relationships wouldn't exist. That's not how they were, they were rational young people whose hearts and minds were working together and at this very moment, this very moment in time, they felt and thought they were making the right decision. At this very moment, it occurred to them…"Do we date other people?" If asked about their relationship, what would they say? They had to really think about this. This is serious. They understood sacrifice, heart and mind, but the thought of them in another relationship, holding someone else's hand, was too much to think about right now. Those thoughts begin to overtake their emotions. Would they remain a couple in theory meaning together but don't talk, hangout or go out on dates together? This decision hit them hard and left many questions unanswered. Just as they got up and got ready to go, they heard Christmas music and they realized Christmas would soon be here…. This was probably the worst day of their young lives……

As they left the park and returned home, they felt like they were leaving a piece of themselves at the park. They would remember this day, they would remember where they sat and they would remember their decision. As they returned to their families to share the decision, each felt strangely more mature, like they were an adult but they were not. They were just 2 kids that made a very mature decision, a decision that they thought was best for their present and their future. As the news was shared with their families, the parents were extremely supportive of the young couple. They didn't say you made the right decision, rather they listened and they listened. They didn't pry into what was said or the decision-making process, rather they listened and they were there for them as the struggled with this decision. The parents liked them as couple and could possibly see them together for a while but as a parent, you must look at the present as well as the future, which isn't certain. The parents knew that kids, who didn't do well in school, would probably develop other problems or issues and those problems or issues will dominate, distract and ultimately, guide the child down the wrong path. What the parents didn't know was what would be the immediate and long-term outcomes of their decision. A broken heart can be a distraction even to the brightest and most focused minds, no one is exempt. The results and outcomes may be same if they stayed together. The parents tried not to reflect back to when their hearts were broken in previous relationships but it is hard not to think about them. They had a really good idea of what their kids must be going through as no one forgets a broken heart, no one...No one forgets how they got a scar...no one...the heart never forgets and the heart will not let the person forget.

Day One, Sunday, the day after the break up...... Leyla and Aaron woke and felt weird, and if a poem had been written, it would probably be:

I feel bland, and invisible
I have lost my way
No one can see inside me
And if it continues, tomorrow will feel like today
Numb both mentally and physically
Stressed and frustrated
And down a little bit spiritually
Everything that is going on in my life
Is nothing I can't handle
I'm trying to be specific with my feelings
Not just sit and ramble
I never had this feeling before
Although I know where it came from
Something major happened to me
That caused these feelings be summoned
Time brings about a change
And it has brought change in me
I must be strong and weather the storm
To control where I want to be

"Now what", they both thought. If they made the right decision, why didn't it feel like it or feel good. Today was the first day of the next phase in their young lives..... from their beds, they slowly looked up through watery eyes to see "the" picture......not just any picture.... this picture reminded them of one of the happiest days of their lives....this picture had a name...and its name was Happy Cakes.......

Thank you for reading my book. I hope you enjoyed the book and learned at least one lesson.

Sincerely,

James Williams

You can't get one step closer to accomplishing your goals if you aren't walking and in the direction towards them.- James Williams

SPECIAL THANKS

I would like to thank my beautiful wife Amanda and our four beautiful kids, Dorothy, James, Samantha, and Blaze for their love, support, and inspiration.

Special thank you to Peachtree Ridge High School Art Class for donating all the pictures used in book.

Other Book by the Author

Coach James' Top Coaching Tips
-Published January 2017 and available on Amazon

Contact the Author- James Williams

Email: coachjamesbiz1@gmail.com
Website: coachjames.org
Mailing address:
6555 Sugarloaf Pkwy ST 307-102
Duluth, GA 30097

Made in the USA
Lexington, KY
18 May 2018